What I Have
In Christ

written & illustrated by Darcy Jackson

Published by Fictitious Ink Publishing, Tumbler Ridge, BC, Canada, V0C 2W0

This booklet is devoted to
Lord Jesus Christ and
our Father in heaven.
It is dedicated to my friend
Alanna
who cheers me on!
Thank you for your encouragement.
I love you,
DarcyL

Matthew 6 : 31 - 33
"So do not worry saying,
'What shall we eat?' or
'What shall we drink?' or
'What shall we wear?'
For ... your heavenly Father
knows that you need them.
But, seek first His Kingdom
and His righteousness and
All these things will be given
to you as well.
Therefore,
DO NOT WORRY ABOUT TOMORROW!"

If God is for us, who can be against us? He who did not spare His own Son, but gave Him up for us all - how will He not also, along with Him, graciously give us all things?

ALL THINGS

Romans 8 : 31, 32

Thank You Father God,
I have been given ALL THINGS
in Christ Jesus.

Praise be to the God and Father of our Lord Jesus Christ, who has blessed us in the heavenly realms with every spiritual blessing in Christ.

BLESSINGS

Ephesians 1 : 3

Thank You Father God for every spiritual BLESSING that I have in Christ Jesus!

Then He took the cup, gave thanks and offered it to them saying, "Drink from it, all of you. This is My blood of the covenant which is poured out for many for the forgiveness of sins.

COVENANT

Matthew 26 : 27, 28

6

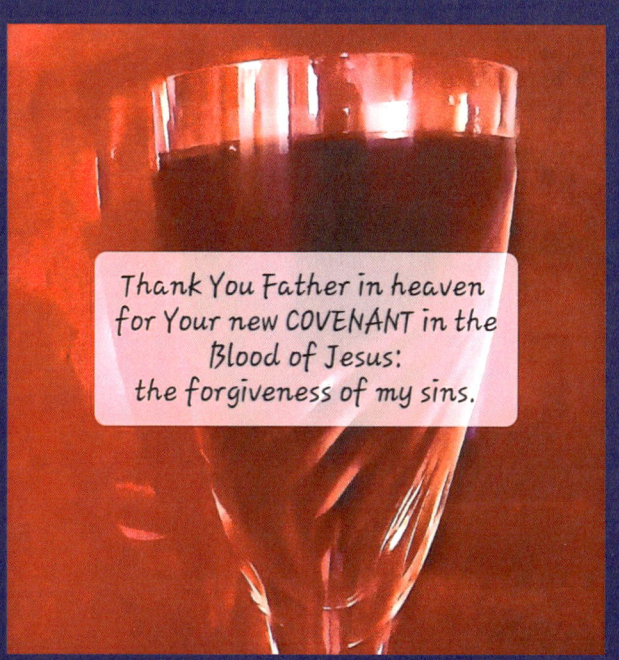

Thank You Father in heaven
for Your new COVENANT in the
Blood of Jesus:
the forgiveness of my sins.

*We speak of God's secret
wisdom that has been hidden and
God destined for our glory before
time began,... as it is written: "No eye
has seen, no ear has heard, no mind
has conceived what God has
prepared for those who love Him".*

DESTINY

1 Corinthians 2 : 7, 9

Thank You Father God for the
DESTINY of glory that
You have prepared for me.

*"My sheep listen to My voice:
I know them and they follow Me.
I give them eternal life and they
shall never perish. No one can
snatch them out of My hand."*

John 10 : 27, 28

ETERNAL LIFE

*"Now this is ETERNAL LIFE:
that they may know You, the
only true God and Jesus Christ,
whom You have sent".*

John 17 : 3

Thank You, my Father, that You
have made Yourself known to me
through Jesus Christ Your Son.
My life is eternal in Your presence.

11

"If you hold to My teaching,
you are really My disciples.
Then you will know the Truth
and the Truth will set you free".

FREEDOM

John 8 : 31, 32

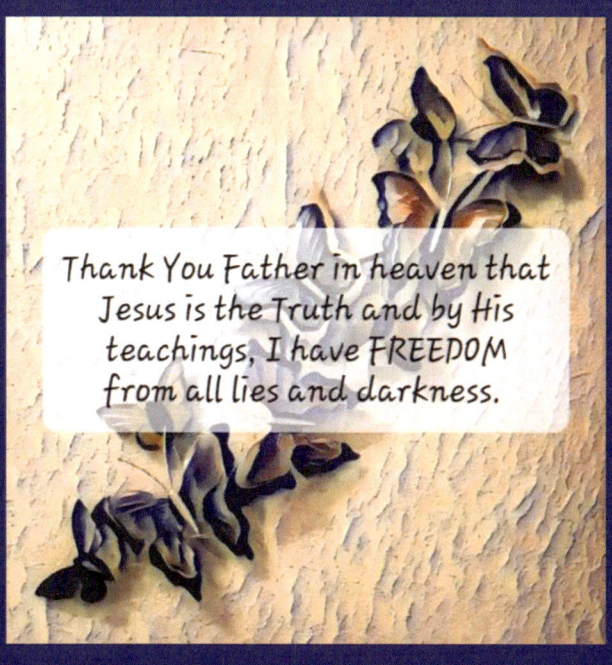

Thank You Father in heaven that
Jesus is the Truth and by His
teachings, I have FREEDOM
from all lies and darkness.

The Word became flesh and
lived for a while among us.
We have seen His glory,
the glory of the Only Begotten
Son, who came from the Father,
full of GRACE and Truth!

GRACE

John 1 : 14

14

Thank You Father for Jesus,
my Savior, so full of GRACE
and Truth for me.

"If you then, though you are evil, know how to give good gifts to your children, how much more will your Father in heaven give the HOLY SPIRIT to those who ask Him!"

HOLY SPIRIT

Luke 11 : 13

16

Thank You Father in heaven
I ask You for Your
HOLY SPIRIT in me.
I receive Your good gift to me
because, by faith, I believe
Your Word and promise to me.

17

Praise be to the God and Father
of our Lord Jesus Christ! In
His great mercy, He has given
us new birth into a living hope
through the resurrection of Jesus
Christ from the dead, and into an
INHERITANCE that can never
perish, spoil or fade -

INHERITANCE

kept in heaven for you; who
through faith are shielded by God's
power until the coming of
salvation that is ready to be
revealed in the last time.

1 Peter 1 : 3 - 5

18

Thank You Father for my INHERITANCE in heaven: my resurrection to an imperishable life in Christ Jesus!

*This day is sacred to our
Lord. Do not grieve,
for the JOY of the Lord
is your strength.*

JOY of the LORD

Nehemiah 8 : 10

20

*I will give you the KEYS of the
Kingdom of heaven; whatever
you bind on earth will be bound
in heaven, and whatever you loose
on earth will be loosed in heaven.*

KINGDOM KEYS

Matthew 16 : 9

Thank You Lord – You have given me KEYS to Your Kingdom, which include repentance, forgiveness and authority over strongholds.

*"Just as the Father raises
the dead and gives them LIFE,
even so the Son gives LIFE to
whom He is pleased to give it".*

John 5 : 21

Thank You Father; in the Name of Your Son Jesus, I have been given LIFE, with hope, power & love.

All this is from God, who
reconciled us to Himself
through Christ and gave us the
MINISTRY of reconciliation:
that God was
reconciling the world to
Himself in Christ, not counting
their sins against them.

MINISTRY

2 Corinthians 5 : 18, 19

Thank You Father for your
message of reconciliation;
a message of hope and
restoration and forgiveness

"A new command I give you:
Love one another!
As I have loved you, so you must
love one another. All people will
know that you are My disciples if
you love one another".

NEW COMMAND

John 13 : 34

Thank You Father for the Love of Christ. I know that You Love me and by Your Love, I am able to love others less selfishly.

I will place on his shoulder
the key to the house of David.
What he opens, no one can shut.
What he shuts, no one can open.

Isaiah 22 : 22

OPEN
OPPORTUNITY

"These are the words of Him
who is holy and true, who holds
the key of David.
What He opens, no one can shut.
What He shuts, no one can open."

Revelation 3 : 7

Thank You Father in heaven.
I know that Jesus holds the key
and He has OPENED
OPPORTUNITIES in my life!

His divine power has given
us everything we need for life and
godliness through our knowledge
of Him who called us by His own
glory and goodness.
Through these He has given us

PROMISES

His very great and precious
PROMISES, so that through them
you may participate in the divine
nature and escape the corruption
in the world caused by evil desires.

2 Peter 1 : 3, 4

Thank You Lord God that all Your PROMISES are 'Yes' in Christ. I believe and receive Your PROMISES in my life.

*For this very reason, make
every effort to add to your faith
goodness, knowledge, self-control,
perseverance, godliness, brotherly
kindness and love.*

QUALITIES

*For if you possess these
QUALITIES in increasing measure,
they will keep you
from being ineffective and
unproductive in your knowledge
of our Lord Jesus Christ.*

Love

Kindness

Godliness

Self-control   Perseverance

Knowledge

Goodness

Faith

2 Peter 1 : 5-8

35

*"Come to Me, all who are
weary and burdened and
I will give you rest.
Take My yoke upon you and
learn from Me.*

REST

*For I AM gentle and humble
in heart, and you will find rest
for your souls. My yoke is easy
and My burden is light."*

Matthew 11 : 28 - 30

Thank You Lord Jesus;
I am resting in You.
I trust in You.
You are gentle and humble
yet strong and powerful!

37

For to us a child is born
to us a SON is given and the
government will be on His
shoulders. And He will be called

SON *of* GOD

Wonderful Counselor,
Mighty God,
Everlasting Father,
Prince of Peace.

Isaiah 9 : 6

38

I love You, Lord Jesus.
Thank You for coming into my
world to save me.
Thank you for giving Your Life
so that my life could have
power, purpose and peace.

*"I AM the Way and the TRUTH and the Life.
No one comes to the Father except through Me.
If you really knew Me, you would know My Father as well.*

TRUTH

John 14 : 6

41

My purpose is that you may be
encouraged in heart and united
in love, so that you may have the
full riches of complete
UNDERSTANDING
in order that you may know the

UNDERSTANDING

mystery of God, namely
Christ, in whom are hidden
all the treasures of wisdom
and knowledge. Amen

Colossians 2 : 2, 3

42

43

*Consider the ravens: they
do not sow or reap, they have
no storeroom or barn; yet God
feeds them.*

VALUE

*And how much more
VALUABLE
you are than birds!*

Luke 12 : 24

44

45

In the beginning was the
WORD, and the WORD was
with God, and the WORD was God.
He was with God in the
beginning. Through Him
all things were made.

WORD of GOD

Without Him nothing was
made that has been made. In
Him was Life, and that Life was
the Light of mankind.

John 1 : 1 - 4

Word of God, I believe that all things were created by You!

47

And now I will show you the
most EXCELLENT WAY.
If I speak in the tongues of men
and angels, but have not love,
I am only a resounding gong or a
clanging cymbal.
If I have the gift of prophecy

EXCELLENT WAY

and can fathom all mysteries
and all knowledge, and if I have
faith that can move mountains,
but have not love,
I am nothing.

1 Corinthians 12 : 31 - 13 : 2

LOVE is patient. LOVE is kind.
It does not envy, it does not boast.
It is not proud. It is not rude.
It is not self-seeking.
It is not easily angered.
It keeps no record of wrongs.
LOVE does not delight in evil
but rejoices with the Truth.
It always protects,
always trusts, always hopes,
always perseveres.
LOVE never fails.

He satisfies my desires with
good things, so that my
YOUTH IS RENEWED
like the eagle's.

YOUTH RENEWED

Psalm 103 : 5

Thank You Lord for my
YOUTH RENEWED
in Your Love.

*You have come to Mount Zion
to the heavenly Jerusalem, the
city of the Living God. You have
come to thousands upon
thousands of angels in joyful
assembly, to the church of the
Firstborn, whose names are
written in heaven.*

ZION

*You have come to God, the
Judge of all people, to the
spirits of righteous ones made
perfect, to Jesus the mediator
of a new covenant
and the sprinkled Blood that
speaks a better Word than the
blood of Abel.*

Hebrews 12 : 22 - 24

Thank You Father for
Your Holy Land.

JERUSALEM

53

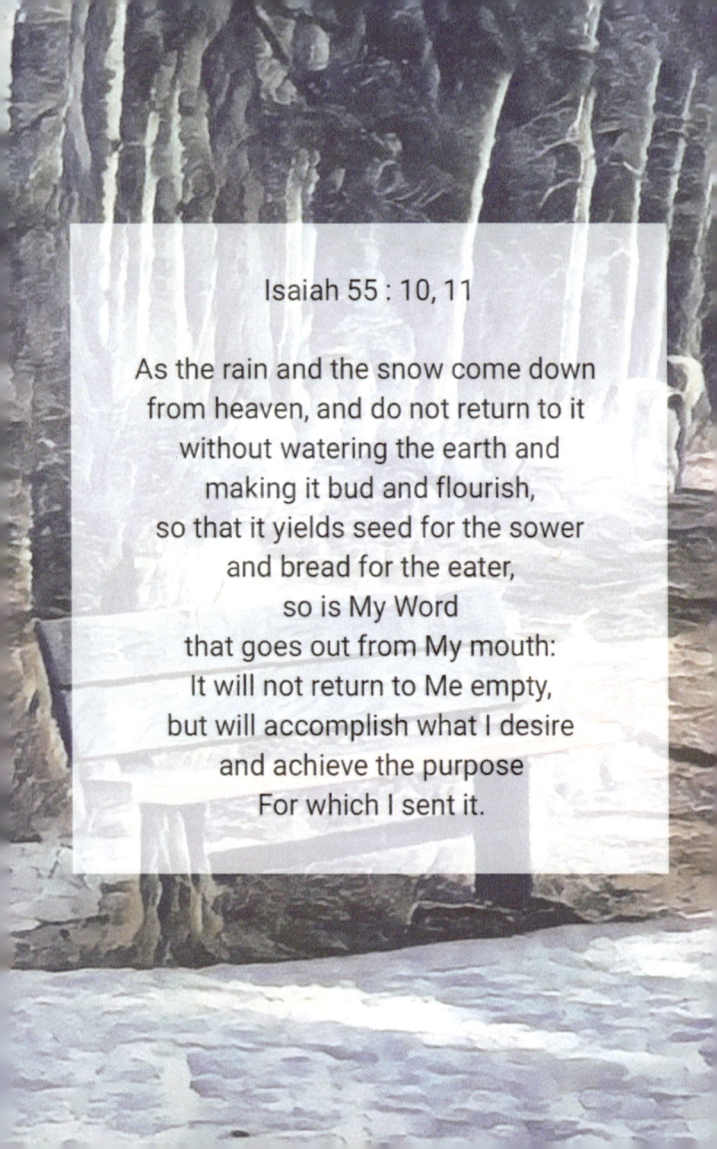

Isaiah 55 : 10, 11

As the rain and the snow come down
from heaven, and do not return to it
without watering the earth and
making it bud and flourish,
so that it yields seed for the sower
and bread for the eater,
so is My Word
that goes out from My mouth:
It will not return to Me empty,
but will accomplish what I desire
and achieve the purpose
For which I sent it.

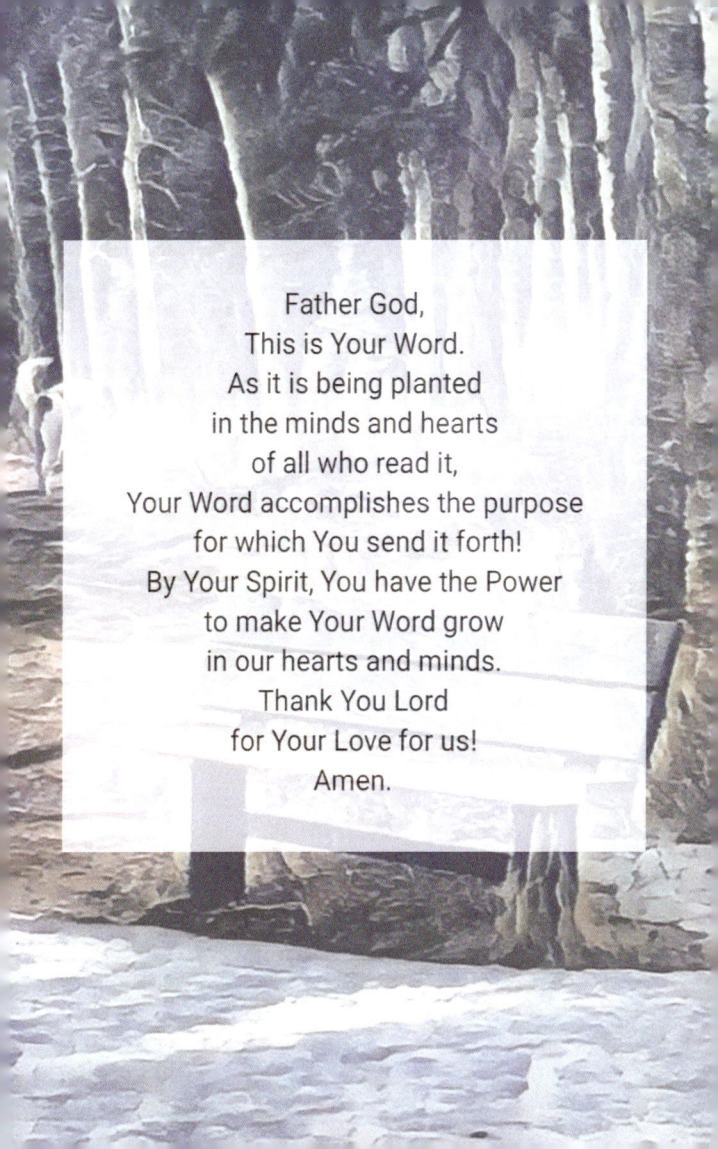

Father God,
This is Your Word.
As it is being planted
in the minds and hearts
of all who read it,
Your Word accomplishes the purpose
for which You send it forth!
By Your Spirit, You have the Power
to make Your Word grow
in our hearts and minds.
Thank You Lord
for Your Love for us!
Amen.

More in the series!

We hope you found this inspirational pocketbook uplifting. The simple affirmative statements, illustrations, and scriptures were prayerfully compiled by the author to bring you strength and peace.

Plus, there are more books in the series! They'd make a beautiful gift for someone you love. Available at select bookstores and online. God bless!

If you enjoyed this book, please consider leaving a positive rating or review.

www.ingramcontent.com/pod-product-compliance
Lightning Source LLC
Chambersburg PA
CBRC090835120626
46547CB00011B/698